# Use The Power Of Arguing To Win Your Next Negotiation

*How To Develop The Skill Of Effective Arguing In A Negotiation In Order To Get The Best Possible Outcome*

*"Practical, proven techniques that will help you get the best deal possible out of your next negotiation"*

**Dr. Jim Anderson**

Published by:
Blue Elephant Consulting
Tampa, Florida

Printed in the United States of America

Library of Congress Control Number:  xxx

ISBN-13:  978-1540323170

ISBN-10:  154032317X

**Warning – Disclaimer**

The purpose of this book is to educate and entertain. This book does not promise or guarantee that anyone following the ideas, tips, suggestions, techniques or strategies will be successful. The author, publisher and distributor(s) shall have neither liability nor responsibility to anyone with respect to any loss or damage caused, or alleged to be caused, directly or indirectly by the information contained in this book.

# Recent Books By The Author

## Product Management

- Product Development Lessons For Product Managers: How Product Managers Can Create Successful Products

- Customer Lessons For Product Managers: Techniques For Product Managers To Better Understand What Their Customers Really Want

## Public Speaking

- Delivering Excellence: How To Give Presentations That Make A Difference: Presentation techniques that will transform a speech into a memorable event

- How To Rehearse In Order To Give The Perfect Speech: How to effectively rehearse your next speech to that your message be remembered forever!

## CIO Skills

- What CIOs Need To Know In Order To Successfully Manage An IT Department: Decision Making Skills That Every CIO Needs To Have In Order To Be Able To Make The Right Choices

- How CIOs Can Make Innovation Happen: Tips And Techniques For CIOs To Use In Order To Make Innovation Happen In Their

IT Department

### IT Manager Skills

- Building The Perfect Team: What Staffing Skills Do IT Managers Need?: Tips And Techniques That IT Managers Can Use In Order To Correctly Staff Their Teams

- Secrets Of Effective Leadership For IT Managers: Tips And Techniques That IT Managers Can Use In Order To Develop Leadership Skills

### Negotiating

- Learn How To Argue In Your Next Negotiation: How To Develop The Skill Of Effective Arguing In A Negotiation In Order To Get The Best Possible Outcome

- How To Open Your Next Negotiation: How To Start A Negotiation In Order To Get The Best Possible Outcome

### Miscellaneous

- How To Heal A Broken Leg – Fast!: Understanding how to deal with a broken leg in order to start walking again quickly

- How Software Defined Networking (SDN) Is Going To Change Your World Forever: The Revolution In Network Design And How It Affects You

**Note**: See a complete list of books by Dr. Jim Anderson at the back of this book.

# <u>Acknowledgements</u>

Any book like this one is the result of years of real-world work experience. In my over 25 years of working for 7 different firms, I have met countless fantastic people and I've been mentored by some truly exceptional ones. Although I've probably forgotten some of the people who made me the person that I am today, here is my attempt to finally give them the recognition that they so truly deserve:

- Thomas P. Anderson
- Art Puett
- Bobbi Marshall
- Bob Boggs

**Dr. Jim Anderson**

*This book is dedicated to my wife Lori. None of this would have been possible without her love and support.*

*Thanks for the best years of my life (so far)...!*

# Table Of Contents

# In A Negotiation, Some Arguing Can Be A Good Thing

As individuals we have a tendency to shy away from getting involved in arguments. We view them as being confrontational and filled with emotions. However, when it comes to negotiating and when we have a different view of the world than the other side of the table, it turns out that a little bit of arguing might be just what the doctor ordered.

Every negotiation is a fast flowing affair. This means that a skilled negotiator knows to not make up his or her mind too early on in the negotiations so that they can remain flexible and open to new ideas. If we get backed into a corner during the negotiations, we may consider using threats to work our way out. However, as with everything in life, there are ramifications to using threats.

The good news about a negotiation is that as a negotiator you don't have to be perfect. This means that you are not required to know everything. Additionally, during the negotiation if it suits you, you can act irrationally. Do be careful about coming across as being too smooth of a negotiator because if you do, then nobody will like you.

During a negotiation you'll have many decisions that you'll have to make. Taking the high ground is one that always seems to pay off. Using standards to back up your position can help establish your credibility. To take this one step further, you need to be aware of any applicable regulations and laws that pertain to the issues being negotiated and you need to use them to the fullest extent.

Our goal in any negotiation is to be able to reach a deal that we can live with. In order to make this happen we can do extraordinary things like bringing a purple money to the negotiations. We also have to learn how to deal with any legal intimidation that the other side may throw at us. We'll have to be prepared to stand our ground if the other side tries to raise the stakes or brings experts into the negotiations.

For more information on what it takes to be a great negotiator, check out my blog, The Accidental Negotiator, at:

**www.TheAccidentalNegotiator.com**

Good luck!

- Dr. Jim Anderson

# About The Author

I must confess that I never set out to be a negotiator. When I went to school, I studied Computer Science and thought that I'd get a nice job programming and that would be that. Well, at least part of that plan worked out!

My first job was working for Boeing on their F/A-18 fighter jet program. I spent my days programming fighter jet software in assembly language and I loved it. The U.S. government decided to save some money and went looking for other countries to sell this plane to. This put me into an unfamiliar role: I started to negotiate with foreign military officials and I ended up having to participate in the negotiations for large international deals.

Time moved on and so did I. I found myself working for Siemens, the big German telecommunications company. They were making phone switches and selling them to the seven U.S. phone companies. The problem was that the switches were too complicated. When it came time to negotiate a deal with the customer, the sales teams struggled to create an effective negotiating strategy. I was called in to bridge the world between the product functionality and the business impacts as they related to the negotiations.

I've spent over 25 years working as a negotiator for both big companies and startups. This has given me an opportunity to learn what it takes to both plan and execute negotiations of all sizes. When it comes to negotiations, I've pretty much been there, done that.

I now live in Tampa Florida where I spend my time managing my consulting business, Blue Elephant Consulting, teaching college courses at the University of South Florida, and traveling to work with companies like yours to share the knowledge that I have about how to prepare for and execute successful negotiations.

I'm always available to answer questions and I can be reached at:

Dr. Jim Anderson
Blue Elephant Consulting
Email: jim@BlueElephantConsulting.com
Facebook: http://goo.gl/1TVoK
Web: **www.BlueElephantConsulting.com**

**"Unforgettable communication skills that will set your ideas free..."**

# Create An Effective Negotiating Team At Your Company!

Dr. Jim Anderson is available to provide training and coaching on the topics that are the most important to people who have to negotiate: how can my team effectively prepare for and execute a successful negotiation that will get us what we both want and need?

Dr. Anderson believes that in order to both learn and remember what he says, audiences need to laugh. Each one of his speeches is full of fun and humor so that what he says "sticks" with everyone.

### Dr. Anderson's Negotiating Training Includes:

1.  How to plan for a negotiation: what information do you| need and where can you find it?

2.  What's the best way to explore how a deal can be created during a negotiation?

3.  How can you bring a negotiation to a close without giving in to the other side?

Dr. Jim Anderson works with over 100 customers per year. To invite Dr. Anderson to work with you, contact him at:

**Phone: 813-418-6970** or
**Email: jim@BlueElephantConsulting.com**

Blue
Elephant
Consulting

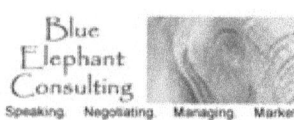

Speaking  Negotiating  Managing  Market

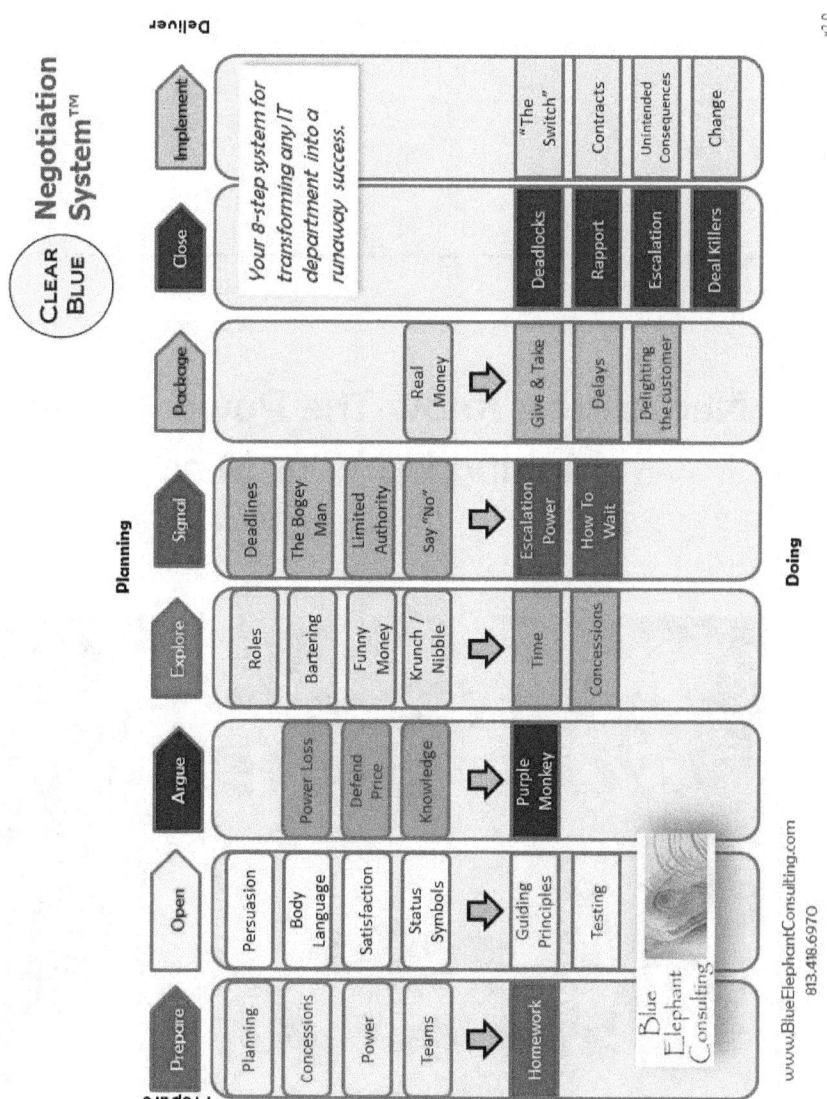

The **Clear Blue Negotiation System™** has been created to provide negotiators with a clear roadmap for how to manage a successful negotiation. This system shows negotiators what needs to be done and in what order to do it.

# Chapter 1

---

## Negotiators Know The Power Of Not Making Up Your Mind

# Chapter 1: Negotiators Know The Power Of Not Making Up Your Mind

I hate to negotiate with people who **don't know how to negotiate**. Knowing this you might think that I'm always expecting the other side to be on top of things, know what they want and have a plan on how they are going to get there. It turns out that you'd be wrong – sometimes not being able to make up your mind is more powerful than knowing where you are going.

## The Power Of Not Knowing

The concept of **not knowing what you want to do** or where you want to go seems to go against the grain of how we like to picture ourselves as negotiators. Instead, we like to see ourselves as bold and confident – knowing where we're going to go even before we get there.

However, what we forget is that every sales negotiation is **a stressful situation**. Any decisions that we make during a negotiation are decisions that we'll be making under pressure – and all too often those types of decisions are bad decisions.

A lot of people don't realize just how much effort goes into not making your mind up. It's actually quite easy to focus on one path of action. Not selecting where you want to go is **much harder**.

## How To Use Indecision To Your Advantage

So maybe not being able to make up your mind is a good thing? In some ways the answer to this question is yes, it can put you into **a more powerful position** when you are negotiating.

One of the biggest benefits of not being able to make up your mind during a negotiation is that **you are in no position to reach a deal**. This means that if the other side wants to settle quickly, then they are going to have to be the ones who make concessions to move both sides close to close.

This also means that you get to control the flow of time. You cannot make up your mind for as long as you want to – you're in charge of that. This can end up **frustrating the other side of the table** and once again this may lead them to making even more concessions just because they want the negotiations to be over and done with!

## What All Of This Means For You

One of the big secrets that most negotiators who are just starting out don't realize is that **a bit of indecision** can be a powerful tool during a negotiation. You'd think that knowing exactly what you want to be doing and where you want the negotiations to be heading would be necessary, but it isn't.

The power that comes from being indecisive comes from the simple fact that **you can't reach a deal with the other side** because you don't really know what you want. This means that the other side can't force you to do something that you don't want to – you don't know enough to make a mistake. This is going to result in the other side making more concessions to you just to keep things moving along.

Despite what your mother may have told you while you were growing up, the brightest people don't always finish first. Sometimes when we don't know what we want to do we can end up **coming out ahead!**

# Chapter 2

---

# 6 Things A Sales Negotiator Needs To Know About Using Threats During A Negotiation

# Chapter 2: 6 Things A Sales Negotiator Needs To Know About Using Threats During A Negotiation

Who doesn't like to **use a threat during sales negotiations** every so often? Threats are yet another one of the negotiation styles and negotiating techniques that we can use. It's like a big stick that you can haul out and set on the table. There it sits, out where everyone can see it and the other side of the table knows what you could do with it if you wanted to. It turns out that that big stick has some consequences that you need to be aware of.

## Threats Are Not Without Consequences

Every negotiation that you are involved in will have the possibility of at least one threat involved in it. Give it some thought – every negotiation has the possibility of **ending in deadlock** as one possible outcome – that's a threat!

When you decide to use a threat of either taking or not taking some action, you need to understand that with a threat comes both **intended and unintended consequences**. What makes a threat really powerful is if the other side decides that they will either gain or lose by believing your threat.

6 Things That You Need To Know About Using Threats In Negotiations

If you aren't careful, the use of threats during your next negotiation **can result in hostility**. Not only that, but they can also result in unintended consequences for you. Because threats are such a tricky weapon to use, here are 6 things that you need to know in order to use threats correctly:

1.  **Credibility Counts:** Your threats won't have any impact on the other side if you aren't going to be seen as being willing to carry them out. We see this all the time around us when we see parents making big threats that they have no intention of ever carrying out to their children in order to get them to behave.

2.  **The Threat Has To Match The Issue:** We're talking about proportionality here. The threat has to match what is being negotiated. If you are trying to get the other side to agree to a small request, then don't use a huge threat to nudge them to give in.

3.  **No Threats Without Backing:** Make sure that your organization is going to back you up on your threat. If the other side of the table knows that they can just go around you and get what they want, then your threat has no teeth.

4.  **Threats Linger:** Before you use a threat, you need to realize that a threat can linger as part of the negotiation process long after you use it. The other side of the table may become angry at having been threatened and may be looking for ways to get revenge later on in the negotiations.

5.  **Threats Change Relationships:** If you have a preexisting relationship with the other side of the table, using threats may forever change that relationship. You need to evaluate whether it's going to be worth it to use the threat.

6.  **Threats Can Get Away From You:** Once you've made a threat during a negotiation, you can't take it back. A threat that has been released into the wild can easily

get away from you and may get out of control. How the other side reacts to your threat may be far beyond what you had anticipated.

## What All Of This Means For You

Threats are a part of every sales negotiation no matter if we want them to be or not. They should almost be part of the negotiation definition. They have a role to play even in a principled negotiation. The key thing that every negotiator needs to realize is that **threats have consequences** that you need to be aware of.

If you make the decision to use a threat during your next negotiation, then you need to **take certain precautions**. These include being credible, making your threats proportional, making sure that you have backing, and understanding that the use of threats has long-term consequences.

In order to be a successful negotiator, we need to be able to make use of every negotiating tool that is available to us. This can include the use of threats. Keep in mind that as powerful as a threat may be, threats do come with some **significant consequences** that you need to be aware of. Keep these in mind and you'll have yet another powerful tool at your disposal.

# Chapter 3

---

# Sales Negotiators Know That They Don't Have To be A Know-It-All

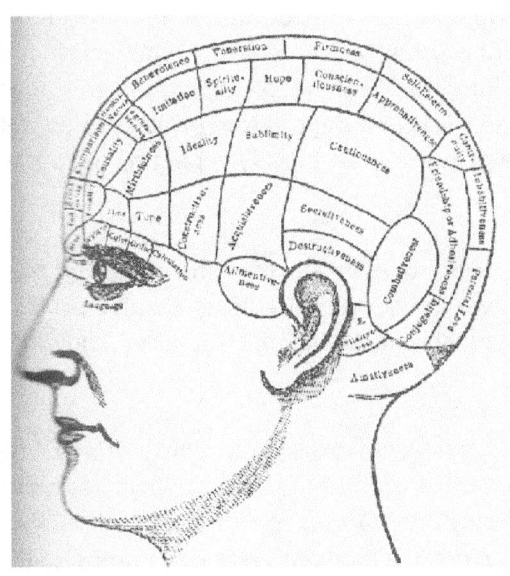

# Chapter 3: Sales Negotiators Know That They Don't Have To be A Know-It-All

Can you remember back to when you were in school? At the end of the term in each class there would be a big test that would determine if you had learned what had been taught to you. You'd do all of your homework and then you'd take extra time to study for the test hoping that most of that information would stay in your head long enough for you to pass the test. Well good news, sales negotiations are not like school tests – **you don't have to know everything in order to do just fine**.

## Why We Think That We Need To Know Everything

When something is being negotiated, for some odd reason we place **an extra burden on ourselves**: we believe that we need to know everything that there is to know about this negotiation. What we forget is that a negotiation process is just that – a process. The other side isn't really expecting us to know everything.

Problems can pop up if we start **feeling obligated to provide an answer** to every question that gets asked. In a principled negotiation you should feel comfortable not knowing everything.

In fact, if you ever get involved in a negotiation in which the person on the other side of the table **always has an answer for every question that you ask**, consider yourself lucky. What's going to happen is that they are going to end up talking too much as they struggle to answer all of your questions and they will end up revealing too much.

## What To Do When You Just Don't Know The Answer

All of this, of course, leads to the big question. What should you do when **you don't know the answer** to something that comes up during a sales negotiation? If someone asked you for a negotiation definition, I think that your answer would be to tell them that a negotiation is a process by which agreement is reached. Part of this process is the asking and answering of questions.

When one of these questions is asked of you and you don't know the answer, this is the time for you to be straightforward with the other side and simply say **"I don't know"**. You'll need to follow this up by saying "I'll have to get back to you on that." This type of response is expected and you won't lose any face by using it.

Keep in mind that telling the other side that you don't know the answer to a question that they have asked doesn't necessarily mean that you don't know the answer. It is perfectly permissible **to not share an answer that you do know** with the other side. Additionally, there will be times that you may want to share only part of the information that you know, or perhaps you'll just want to put off sharing what you know until later in the sales negotiation process.

## What All Of This Means For You

As sales negotiators we often like to think of ourselves as **being all knowing**. The reality is actually quite different – there is a lot out there that we just don't know.

During a negotiation we need to have the confidence in ourselves to be able to **speak up when we don't know the answer to something**. In fact, you might know the answer but that doesn't mean that you have to answer a question. There is no shame in telling the other side that you are going to have to check on something or do some research before you'll be able to answer their question.

Having the self-confidence to not have to have all of the answers is one of the **great negotiating styles** that is all too often overlooked. We all have different negotiation styles, but not pretending to have all of the answer is one style that we should all adopt.

# Chapter 4

---

# Sales Negotiators Know That It's Ok To Be Irrational

# Chapter 4: Sales Negotiators Know That It's Ok To Be Irrational

How do you view yourself when you are conducting a negotiation? Do you see yourself as poised, confident, and above all rational? I think that most of us see ourselves this way. However, it turns out that **we might be missing something here** – there is a real power in being irrational sometimes…

## Just What Does Irrationality Look Like During A Negotiation?

So let's think about this for a moment: do we really know what rational people look like? I mean, **we think that we do**. We believe that we have conversations with them each and every day. They seem to keep their voices in a low conversational tone, they listen quietly when you are talking to them and they respond with carefully thought out responses to what you've just said.

So if we can all agree on what **the negotiation style** of a rational negotiator is, it does bring up the question of just exactly what does the negotiating technique of an irrational negotiator look like?

The answer is that it looks pretty much like what you would expect it to look like. Irrational behavior takes on **many different forms** during a sales negotiations. The first is that you start to reject what the other side of the table says without having a good reason. Another sign that you may be an irrational negotiator is if you start to express a lot of emotions during the negotiations.

Irrationality can **take on many different forms**. The other side may present you with very rational arguments, but you don't have to agree with them. You have a number of different choices: you can be partly logical, illogical, even go all the way and be illogical.

## How Powerful Is Irrationality?

I can almost hear you saying "Why should I be irrational during a sales negotiation?" In fact, if I want to engage in principled negotiation **should I even consider using irrational negotiations?** When we look at the negotiation definition that we all use, we realize that the best way to look at irrationality is that it is just another tool that needs to be in everone's negotiator's toolkit.

The other side of the table will be spending the entire time that you are negotiating **trying to read your mind**. Trying to figure out what your next step is going to be. When you start to work some irrationality into your negotiation process, you will confuse them.

This is **a powerful negotiating technique**; however, you may struggle to pull it off. It really comes down to what your natural negotiating style is. If you are a highly logical person who rarely shows any emotion during a negotiation, then you may struggle to start to incorporate irrational behavior into your negotiations.

## What Does All Of This Mean For You?

In the classic sci-fi TV show "Star Trek", the bad guys have a cloaking device that allows their spacecraft to disappear. As a sales negotiator it turns out that you have your own form of **a cloaking device**: the power of behaving irrationally.

The other side of the table will always be trying to read your mind and **pre-anticipate what your next move is going to be**.

27

Using your ability to be illogical can throw off the other side. Being illogical means that at times you become unreasonable, you start to show a great deal of emotion or you simply don't agree with what they have presented, no matter how clear and logical it is.

In order to have successful negotiations, you need to be able to **take on multiple identities** during a negotiation. Becoming an illogical negotiator is one such identity and the sooner you learn to use your illogical powers, the sooner you'll be on your way to closing more deals successfully.

# Chapter 5

---

# Nobody Likes A Good Negotiator

# Chapter 5: Nobody Likes A Good Negotiator

So it turns out that one of the **key personality characteristics** that may have gotten you this far in your career may actually be hindering your ability to negotiate. Yep, in the world of negotiating, there's no place for a nice guy.

## It's All About Conflict

We spend a lot of time talking about how we'd like each and every one of our negotiating sessions to result in a "win-win" outcome. That's all very nice. No matter what negotiation styles you use or what negotiating techniques you employ during a negotiation, **you need to be disliked by the other side**.

This may seem a bit harsh, but if I had to come up with a negotiation definition, I would have to call it "controlled conflict". That means that your job is to **reach an agreement with the other side**, not to be liked by them.

The reason that this is such a big deal is simply because deep down inside, we all have **a fundamental need** to be liked. As we conduct our principled negotiation we expect that if we go to the effort of liking the other side of the table, they will like us and everyone will be able to reach that "win-win" finish line. Sadly, real life doesn't work that way.

Instead, if you have too much of a need to be liked, there is a very good chance the that other side of the table will pick up on this and will **use it against you**. At different times they may make you feel as though you are their best friend as they attempt to get you to agree to what they want. At other times they may appear to be cold and distant in order to make you search for ways to bring them back close to you by giving in to their demands.

Give it up. In the world of negotiations you can either be liked by the other side or **you can be a successful negotiator** – you can only have one, please choose now.

## Why It's Ok To Not Be A Nice Guy (or Girl)

As counter-intuitive as this may seem, during the negotiation process you don't have to worry about what the other side thinks about you. In fact, if you can find a way to not spend any time thinking about what they think of you, **you'll be much better off**.

If you spend too much time thinking about how you are being viewed, it will take time away from what you should be focused on: **reaching the best deal**. When the other side appears to be hostile and makes attacks that almost seem to be personal affronts, if we are worrying about how the other side views us then we'll be distracted from crafting an effective response.

Instead, **focus on what's being negotiated**. You want the other side of the table to not like you – your goal is not to be their friend during the negotiation. Depending on what's being negotiated, the negotiations could drag on for quite some time. Allowing the other side to not like you takes an enormous burden off of your shoulders and allows you to focus on what's really important: reaching a deal.

## What All Of This Means For You

We would all like to be liked by everyone that we come into contact with. The problem with this is that during a sales negotiation, this need to be liked can turn into **a significant handicap**. We need to get over it.

If you can allow yourself to not care how the other side of the table is viewing you during a negotiation, you will be in **a much**

**stronger position**. Realizing that if you allow the other side to influence how you feel that they feel about you then they will be able to get you to make concessions that you wouldn't normally have made. Instead, put aside your need to be liked during the negotiation and instead focus on reaching the best deal possible.

It's not easy to not care how someone feels about you. However, when you are in the middle of negotiating a big deal **you need to be able to do this**. There will be time to mend fences and build bridges with the other side of the negotiating table – after you have successfully reached a deal with them!

# Chapter 6

---

# Negotiators Know That You Can Only Win By Taking The High Ground

# Chapter 6: Negotiators Know That You Can Only Win By Taking The High Ground

When it comes to how you want to conduct your next negotiation, there are an almost limitless number of ways to go about doing it. Some of them are above board and some of them are downright sneaky. I'm going to suggest that if you want to walk away from the negotiating table with a deal that both sides are going to feel good about, then **you're going to have to take the high ground…**

## What Is The "High Ground" And Why You Should Care

In order to reach the outcome of a negotiation that you want to, you need to be in the driver's seat – you need to be **controlling the direction that the negotiation takes**. The challenge here is that the other side of the table will be trying to do exactly the same thing at the same time.

During the negotiation process, you will take positions and you will ask the other side to make concessions to you. As you might well expect, they are probably not going to be all that interested in making those concessions to you. Your negotiating skills will have to come into play as you attempt to convince them to **adopt your views** and make concessions.

This process can either be easy or hard to do. You can make it much easier on yourself if you choose at the outset of the negotiating session **to take the high ground**. This isn't one of the negotiating techniques that we are talking about. Rather it's more a part of an overall principled negotiation philosophy.

Taking the high ground during a negotiation means that instead of trying to bully or verbally overpower the other side of the table, instead you rely on solid evidence in the form of both **logic and facts**. It's not all about you, rather the reason that the other side should adopt your viewpoint is because of the compelling evidence that shows that it really is the correct way to go.

## How To Reach The High Ground

Realizing that the high ground is the correct way to go during a negotiation and then actually taking it are two completely different things. Any negotiation definition tells you that you are going to have conflict with the other side during the negotiation and staying on the high ground **can be a difficult thing to do**.

There are many negotiation styles that you can choose from when you are starting your next negotiation; however the following **four components** must always be included in what you do in order to allow you to keep the high ground:

1. **Have A Solid Direction: You have got to know where you are going. Having a strong sense of where you want the negotiations to lead to is key to allowing you to retain the high ground.**

2. **Having History On Your Side:** Do your homework before the negotiation and be able to point out how your positions are simply a continuation of what has been agreed to by the other side in the past.

3. **Love That Logic:** The nice thing about logic is that people can't really argue with it. Take the time to think out your positions and then present them in a logical

fashion to the other side.

4. **Use Standards:** If somebody else has established a standard then make sure that your proposal is supported by this standard and make sure that you tell the other side this.

## What All Of This Means For You

Negotiating can be a tough job. As you enter a negotiation you need to make a decision about **how you want to get to the end**. There are a lot of different ways to get there, some are above board and a whole bunch are not.

Experienced negotiators know that **sticking to the high ground** is the best way to conduct a negotiation. Using solid backup material consisting of factual evidence and well-though out logic allows you to convince the other side of the table that you really are looking to strike a deal with them.

Negotiators can be tempted to forego the high ground if they find themselves in a rush – they just need to **get a deal done quickly**. However, it's been proven time after time that if you don't take the high ground during your negotiations, the deal that you negotiated won't be one that either side will want to live with.

# Chapter 7

## Why The Standard Answer Can Help A Negotiator Close The Deal

## Chapter 7: Why The Standard Answer Can Help A Negotiator Close The Deal

Magical mind control powers. That's what every sales negotiator would like to have. The ability to **bend the other side of the table's mind to your way of thinking** would be the set of negotiation styles or negotiating techniques that would make life so much easier. Sadly, I don't believe that such powers exist. However, there is something that comes pretty close – standards.

## What Standards Are And Where You Can Find Them

So right off the bat I guess we should tackle the big question: **just what the heck is a "standard"?** Standards are documented ways of going about doing something that were created by someone else. Note that I didn't say that a standard is recognized as an official source by anyone in particular nor did I say that it was created by a person who is well regarded in a particular field. Don't worry, using standards is still a part of conducting a principled negotiation!

A standard is simply that: **documentation about something**. The important thing from your point of view is that during a negotiation when you introduce a standard into the discussion that both sides start to treat the standard as the ultimate source of information. Using standards should almost be considered part of the negotiation definition.

If you are preparing for a negotiation and you find that there is no existing standard that will support your position, then it may be time for you to **create your own standard**. Even if you don't create the standard, you can at least have someone within your company create it for you. Remember that who creates a standard doesn't really matter, it's just the simple fact that the standard exists that gives it its power.

## How To Use Standards To Get Your Way In A Negotiation

Once you have the standards that you're going to need in order to conduct a successful negotiation, you need to understand how to use them as part of the negotiation process. The real power from a standard comes from the fact that **it now equips you with legitimacy**.

During the negotiations you can refer to the standards and say things like "I've got to stay within these standards, that's what my management has told me to do." The other side of the table might not like this, **but what can they do?**

Just by having a standard, you can make it easier for the other side **to agree to go along with the proposals that you are making**. The standards provide you with an air of legitimacy and they help to guide the other side to reaching the decision that you really want them to make.

## What All Of This Means For You

As a negotiator you are always looking for **new ways to gain legitimacy** in the eyes of the other side of the table. You really want to find ways to make your way of seeing the world their way too so that a negotiated deal is that much easier to reach.

Standards that you bring to the table can provide you with the support that you are looking for. These standards don't have to be fancy internationally recognized standards. Standards that have been developed by your company (perhaps just for this negotiation!) often have as much weight. Simply by having a standard, you can **reduce the amount of push-back** that the other side will give to your proposals.

Take the time to plan your next negotiation. Look for ways to boost your position by **the introduction of one or more standards**. When the time is right, bring them to the table and defer to them. You may be amazed at just how powerful the right standard at the right time can be!

# Chapter 8

## Sales Negotiators Need To Know How To Use Regulations And Laws To Reach A Deal

# Chapter 8: Sales Negotiators Need To Know How To Use Regulations And Laws To Reach A Deal

I can only speak for myself, but when I'm headed into a negotiation I like to have **as much freedom to do things as possible**. That's why I tend to shudder when I discover that there are regulations or even laws that are going to impact the negotiations. However, maybe I'm not looking at the complete picture.

## How Regulations And Laws Can Harm A Negotiation

When we enter a negotiation, one of the things that we need to know even before we sit down is just exactly who is in the room? Sure there are the people who are physically there, but are there **requirements and restrictions** placed on either side of the table by others? This can have a big impact on the negotiation styles and the negotiating techniques that we can use.

When regulations and laws get involved, that negotiating room can get pretty crowded, pretty quickly. When we have to negotiate with these kinds of restrictions, all of a sudden **our options start to narrow**. I for one start to fell rather constrained. The negotiation definition is altered in these negotiating situations.

One of the biggest challenges that I've encountered to conducting principled negotiation is when the laws that you are negotiating under require you to **reveal more information to the other side than you normally would**. This tends to screw up the whole negotiation process for me. A great example of this is when you are negotiating with the government – after all, they get to make up the laws. Often times you'll find that you are required to reveal elements of your product or services' costs that you normally would not share with the other side of the table. Ouch!

## How Regulations And Laws Can Help A Negotiation

Having regulations and laws come and sit at the negotiating table with you is not always a bad thing. If it turns out that **they are working for you**, then this can actually be a good thing.

The key here is to **do your homework** before you start any negotiation. What you need to be looking for are those regulations, statutes, rules or laws that support your negotiating position. The more of these that you are able to find, the easier it is going to be to get the other side to come around to agreeing with your position.

In addition to helping you with the other side of the table, regulations and laws **can help you better manage your own company**. When others in your company see the constraints that you are operating under, they will be more likely to put their support behind your negotiating positions and provide you with the support that you'll need to be successful.

## What All Of This Means For You

Negotiations can be tricky to do well. When regulations and laws get involved, things **can become a great deal more challenging**. Sales negotiators need to understand how to work in these situations.

These conditions can require that a negotiator **reveal more to the other side of the table** than they normally would. It's very important to take the time to understand just exactly what the regulations require you as a negotiator to do.

Depending on exactly what the restrictions are, **they can work in your favor**. If they limit the other side of the table's options, then it may become easier for the other side to agree to your requests and reach the deal that you wanted to have negotiated. In the end, that may make it worth all of the extra effort that these restrictions require.

# Chapter 9

---

# Get What You Want By Bringing A Purple Monkey To Your Next Negotiation

# Chapter 9: Get What You Want By Bringing A Purple Monkey To Your Next Negotiation

How did your last negotiation go? Did you and the other side of the table spend your time working through a long list of demands that the other side had made? Did you end up feeling as though you had negotiated for a very long time? The next time that you prepare for a negotiation, you need to come up with a way to streamline the process so that you can **reach an agreement quickly**. It turns out that you can make this happen by bringing a purple monkey to the negotiations.

## Don't Let The Other Side Control The Negotiation

When you sit down to negotiate, **who's in charge?** I mean, it's either you or them, right? Why let them take charge? Why not seize the reigns of the negotiation process right off the bat and take charge?

If you don't do this, then what can happen? In short order, no matter what negotiation styles or negotiating techniques you are using, you may find yourself spending a lot of time talking about things that you really don't want to be talking about. Things that you don't want to talk about can be broken into two groups: **trivial things and dangerous things**.

Trivial things are those things that show up on the long list of push-backs to your proposal that you get from the other side. It's always very hard to determine which of these items are **real issues**, and which ones have just been brought up so that the other side has some negotiating currency to play around with.

Dangerous things are those issues that you really don't want to have to negotiate about with the other side of the table. These can relate to shortcomings that you know that your offer has, or issues where you have not been given any flexibility by your management. No matter what the cause is, you know that if you have to spend a lot of time discussing these types of issues, **things are not going to go well for you**.

## How A Purple Monkey Can Help You Control The Negotiation

If you want to take control of your next negotiation, then **you need to bring a purple monkey to the table**. No, I'm not suggesting that you go down to the zoo and ask for a loaner — that wouldn't be part of a principled negotiation. Rather, I'm going to suggest that you do a little bit of work before the negotiations start in order to ensure that they go the way that you want them to go.

Here's what you need to do. Take a look at the issue that you're going to be negotiating. Focus on the proposal that you'll be bringing to the table. Now, go ahead and add **an unreasonable request** to your proposal. Something that you know that the other side just won't be able to sit for. Slide it right in there and make sure that nobody removes it before it gets presented to the other side.

This unreasonable request is your **"purple monkey"**. It's so big and unacceptable that it's going to completely capture the other side's attention. They are going to look at that and instantly they are going to start to try to come up with ways to get you to remove it from your proposal.

Oh sure, you will eventually remove it. However, it's going to take a lot of convincing by the other side to get you to do it. The effect of this is that the other side is going to **be distracted** and they're not going to notice all of the trivial things that they would otherwise put on a list to negotiate with you.

Likewise, that purple monkey is going to be so distracting that there is a very good chance that the other side won't think to bring up **the dangerous issues** that you really don't want to talk about. Simply by bringing the purple monkey to the table, you've taken control of the negotiation and you've steered it in the direction that you wanted it to go.

## What All Of This Means For You

In any negotiations, there are going to be demands placed on you by the other side of the table – there's nothing that you can do about this. However, what you can control is **what those demands are** and how many of them there are.

In order to prevent the other side from creating a long list of items to be discussed over a long period of time, be proactive. When you make your initial proposal to them, **include a purple monkey in it**. This item is one that you know will be completely unacceptable to the other side. In fact, it will completely gain their attention and make them insist that it be removed from your proposal. By causing them to focus on your purple monkey, you'll shorten the list of other items that need to be negotiated.

Although adding this purple monkey technique to your negotiation definition may seem to be simple to do, it turns out that **it is very powerful**. Take control of your next negotiation by spending the time before the negotiation and find out how you can bring your purple monkey to the table so that you can reach a better deal quicker.

# Chapter 10

---

## Legal Intimidation: 5 Ways To Defend Against It

# Chapter 10: Legal Intimidation: 5 Ways To Defend Against It

Hear any good lawyer jokes lately? When we are negotiating we like to think that we're prepared for almost any possibility. However, there's one thing that can cause the blood of even a seasoned negotiator to run cold: the threat of legal action. All of the negotiation styles and negotiating techniques in the world aren't going to help you now. **What's a negotiator to do?**

## Why We Fear Lawyers So Much

So exactly why do negotiators **fear legal intimidation** so much? It's my opinion that we view the world of the legal system, no matter what country you are working in, as being a bit of a "black box". We don't know how it works. It's not something that can be negotiated away.

The only people who seem to understand the legal system are lawyers. That means that when the other side of the table uses legal intimidation as part of the negotiation process in order to get their way during a negotiation, **they'll bring in the lawyers**.

In today's hurry-up world, the use of legal intimidation brings with it **two threats**. The first is that it's going to cost a lot of money to resolve. Lawyers generally get paid by the hour and they can charge anywhere from $350 -$1,000 per hour. You can see how things can get very expensive very quickly.

The other implied threat that any sort of legal intimidation brings with it is the threat of **slowing the whole negotiation process down**. Legal action involves courts, paperwork, and a lot of time to prepare for. This all takes away from the business of negotiating and that can't be a good thing.

# How You Can Defend Against Legal Intimidation

If we can all agree that legal intimidation is a big scary thing, this naturally leads to the next question: what can a negotiator do about it? Just threat of legal action by the other side can sometimes tip the negotiations in their favor and we need to **find a way to fight back**.

Here are **5 ways** that any negotiator can respond in a powerful fashion when the other side starts to use legal intimidation:

1. **Understand That They Are Buffing:** Although the threat of taking legal action sounds serious, we need to understand that more often than not it's just talk on the other side's part. Legal action costs money, potentially a lot of money, and so just because they are making threats doesn't mean that they're actually going to do anything.

2. **Financially Prepare:** The effectiveness of using legal intimidation against you can be minimized if you have already factored it into your negotiation preparations. This can be as simple as determining how much going to court would cost and making sure that you have a way to get the funds that you would need if it comes to that.

3. **Consider Mediation:** Going to court should be considered to be a last resort. A much better way to resolve any issues that appear to be forcing both sides into making a courtroom appearance would be to sit down with a mediator. This is always a good idea because it just might prevent a costly legal battle.

4. **Get Good Legal Advice:** When it comes to legal matters, you don't know what you don't know. This means that you really need to have access to a lawyer if for no

other reason than to ask them questions as your negotiations proceed. The fancy term for this is to place a lawyer "on retainer" where you pay them money to be available to help you out.

5.  **Pick The Best:** If all else fails and you find yourself headed off to court, then you need to get yourself the best lawyer that your money can buy. You really want to take the time and do some research here: have they dealt with this type of case before and what was the outcome? Do your homework and choose wisely — there's a lot riding on your decision.

## What All Of This Means For You

I think that we can all agree on one thing: **lawyers are scary**. However, when we are negotiating we need to understand that the other side will use legal intimidation in order to get their way — it has almost become part of the negotiation definition. We need to be prepared.

Realistically, we need to understand that going to court is expensive and time consuming for everyone. Therefore, most of the time legal threats are just that — threats. However, we need to **take steps to defend ourselves**. We can do this by contacting a lawyer and having them ready if things go badly for us.

When it comes to legal intimidation, **fighting back is possible** and needs to part of your principled negotiation techniques. You just need to know the rules of the game and then come to your next negotiation prepared for what the other side may legally throw at you. Keep in mind, justice is blind…!

# Chapter 11

---

## Negotiators Need To Learn How To Deal With Experts

# Chapter 11: Negotiators Need To Learn How To Deal With Experts

So let's think about your next negotiating session. There you are and everything is going along quite nicely. You are making your points and the other side doesn't seem to be objecting to them too much. All of a sudden another person arrives and joins the other side of the table. They are introduced as **an expert** and they then proceed to tear big holes in the justifications that you had given for the deal that you were proposing. Dang it – done in by an expert once again.

## Why Experts Cause Us So Much Trouble

You are a bright, smart negotiator. Why does the arrival of an expert at a negotiating session cause you so much trouble? What seems to happen is that when an expert shows up, **all of a sudden we shut up**. We are no longer willing to exert ourselves.

What's up with this? It turns out that one of the big problems that we encounter when an expert shows up is that **they speak funny**. It's like they have a completely different vocabulary that they use when they talk about the part of the negotiation that they've been brought in for. All we can do is sit back and take it in – we don't have the same vocabulary.

When we find ourselves in the presence of an expert, we do pretty much anyone else would do – **we become passive**. We really don't want to speak up because we fear looking foolish. The problem with this response to authority is that we can allow the negotiations that we are involved in to slip away from us because we've become quiet.

## How To Handle Experts In A Negotiation

This all leads us to the really big question: what can a negotiator do when the other side brings an expert to a negotiation session? Short of asking them to go away, is there some **magic technique** that we can use to deal with them?

The answer, somewhat surprisingly, is yes. Right off the bat, you need to have a talk with yourself when an expert shows up. What you need to remind yourself about is the simple fact that nobody is **an expert in everything**. In fact, the more that someone knows about something, then the less they probably know about more things.

The other thing that you need to keep in mind is two simple words **"so what?"** Yes, the other person is an expert in some area and you are not. However, if this deal is going to happen, then you are going to have to agree to it. The expert may have many valid points to make, but who cares? At the end of the day it's going to be up to you to either accept or reject what they say. The really neat part about this is that it does not matter if they are correct or not – you can reject what they say even if they are right!

## What All Of This Means For You

Nothing can **screw up** a good negotiation like the arrival of an expert. For some reason when we are in the presence of someone who has been introduced to us as an expert, we freeze up. Our negotiation skills seem to vanish.

The reasons for this differ from negotiator to negotiator, but it's all due to the fact that we don't know how to handle someone who clearly knows a lot more about a subject than we do. What we need to learn to do is to understand that **there are limits** to how much any one expert can know. This coupled with the fact that their opinion won't control the outcome of the negotiations means that you still have the power.

We can't do anything about having experts introduced into a negotiation. However, what we can do is to decide just how influenced by their presence we want to allow ourselves to become. **Minimize their influence over you** and you can still reach a great deal with the other side of the table.

# Chapter 12

## What To Do When The Other Side Tries To Intimidate You By Raising The Stakes

# Chapter 12: What To Do When The Other Side Tries To Intimidate You By Raising The Stakes

Intimidation can take on many forms during the course of a sales negotiation. One of the forms of intimidation that we are all very familiar with is when the other side of the table **starts to raise the stakes**. All of a sudden, what used to be a simple negotiation process suddenly become a lot more important. What's a negotiator to do?

## Why Do They Try To Intimidate Us By Raising The Stakes?

Negotiating is all about power. The more power you have, the better the chances that you will get what you want out of the negotiations. This means that the other side of the table will always be looking for the negotiation styles and negotiating techniques that will provide them with **ways to get more power** while at the same time taking power away from you.

One way to go about doing this is to find ways to intimidate you. Anything that they can do to make their position **seem more threating** to what you are trying to accomplish will make you want to give in to their demands that much faster. This may not be the best example of principled negotiating; however, nobody can argue with the fact that in many cases it's very successful. Many deals have been negotiated using this technique.

One of the classic ways that the other side can seek to intimidate you during your next negotiation is by **raising the stakes**. When they change things or make an offer that all of sudden makes it very expensive for you to say "no", then they have raised the stakes.

## Ways That The Stakes Can Be Raised

There are a lot of different ways to raise the stakes during a negotiation – far too many for me to hope to be able to list them all here. However, we can cover a few of them in order to give you a flavor of **what this tactic looks like**.

One of the classic ways to raise the stakes occurs when you've been negotiating with the other side of the table for a while. You've reached agreement on a number of issues, and then all of a sudden they hit you with either a new demand or they increase their demands in a number of areas. At the same time they tell you that **they are backing away from all of the previous agreements that they have made with you**. Congratulations, the stakes have just been raised.

Another example is when you are already in a business agreement with the other side of the table. If they show up and offer you **a bigger agreement**, but insist that your current agreement will go away if you bid on the bigger agreement is not low enough, then they have just raised the stakes.

## What We Can Do When The Stakes Have Been Raised

The very first thing that you need to understand about the negotiating tactic where the stakes are raised is that **there must be a reason** that the other side is doing this right now. There can be many reasons: this was always their goal, they are running out of time to negotiate, they are close to striking a deal with somebody else, etc.

Ideally, you'll find out **what is motivating them**. This is critical knowledge that can help you to decide what your next steps need to be. However, in many cases this simply won't be possible.

In those cases, you need to plan your next steps carefully. The first thing that you are going to want is time to evaluate the new situation. **Ask for a break in the negotiations**. Next, determine if raising the stakes on your side would cause the other side to back down. If not, then pick apart their position – where do you need to have agreement with them and what issues don't matter as much.

Instead of allowing the other side to present you with **a "take it or leave it" proposal**, come back to the negotiating table and explore which of the issues they are firm on and where they have some flexibility. I suspect that there is one issue that is most important to them and the process of raising the stakes was just designed to get their way on that one issue.

## What All Of This Means For You

In order to get what they want from a negotiation, the other side may resort to using **intimidation tactics**. One of the most common ways to do this is to raise the stakes as you move through the negotiation. This is so common that it's almost a part of the negotiation definition.

There are many different ways that the other side can go about doing this. These include bluffing, changing their mind on previously agreed to agreements, or presenting alternative deals. As negotiators we need to always **be aware of when this type of intimidation starts to happen**. We need to evaluate the risk to them and look for ways that we can raise the stakes for them.

Intimidation by raising the stakes is something that we will all have to deal with during negotiations. Being aware that it's happening is the first step and then knowing how to respond is the second. During your next negotiation, **don't be intimidated** no matter how high the stakes go!

It's from the forge of failure that the steel of success is formed.

Hard Work Does Not Guarantee Success, But Success Does Not Happen Without Hard Work.

- Dr. Jim Anderson

# Create An Effective Negotiating Team At Your Company!

Dr. Jim Anderson is available to provide training and coaching on the topics that are the most important to people who have to negotiate: how can my team effectively prepare for and execute a successful negotiation that will get us what we both want and need?

Dr. Anderson believes that in order to both learn and remember what he says, audiences need to laugh. Each one of his speeches is full of fun and humor so that what he says "sticks" with everyone.

### Dr. Anderson's Negotiating Training Includes:

1. How to plan for a negotiation: what information do you need and where can you find it?

2. What's the best way to explore how a deal can be created during a negotiation?

3. How can you bring a negotiation to a close without giving in to the other side?

Dr. Jim Anderson works with over 100 customers per year. To invite Dr. Anderson to work with you, contact him at:

**Phone: 813-418-6970** or
**Email: jim@BlueElephantConsulting.com**

Blue
Elephant
Consulting

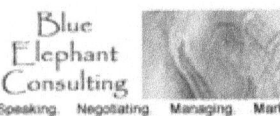

Speaking.  Negotiating.  Managing.  Marketi

12

# Photo Credits:

Cover - Vic
https://www.flickr.com/photos/59632563@N04/


Chapter 1 - Riccardo Cuppini
https://www.flickr.com/photos/cuppini/


Chapter 2 - Backdoor Survival
https://www.flickr.com/photos/backdoorsurvival/


Chapter 3 - Lovelorn Poets
https://www.flickr.com/photos/lovelornpoets/


Chapter 4 - Thomas Hawk
https://www.flickr.com/photos/thomashawk/


Chapter 5 - Kayla Sawyer
https://www.flickr.com/photos/ksawyer/


Chapter 6 - Basheer Tome
https://www.flickr.com/photos/basheertome/

Chapter 7 - pongo 2007
https://www.flickr.com/photos/pongo2007/


Chapter 8 – Eddi
https://www.flickr.com/photos/eddi_07/


Chapter 9 - sunsetgirl creations
https://www.flickr.com/photos/sunsetgirl_creations/


Chapter 10 - Andrew //
https://www.flickr.com/photos/sluys/


Chapter 11 - Graham Lavender
https://www.flickr.com/photos/guybrariang/


Chapter 12 - Jim Surkamp
https://www.flickr.com/photos/jimsurkamp/

# Other Books By
# The Author

## Product Management

- How To Create A Successful Product That Customers Will Want: Techniques For Product Managers To Boost Product Sales And Increase Customer Satisfaction

- What Product Managers Need To Know About World-Class Product Development: How Product Managers Can Create Successful Products

- How Product Managers Can Learn To Understand Their Customers: Techniques For Product Managers To Better Understand What Their Customers Really Want

- Product Management Secrets: Techniques For Product Managers To Boost Product Sales And Increase Customer Satisfaction

- Product Development Lessons For Product Managers: How Product Managers Can Create Successful Products

- Customer Lessons For Product Managers: Techniques For Product Managers To Better Understand What Their Customers Really Want

- Product Failure Lessons For Product Managers: Examples Of Products That Have Failed For Product Managers To Learn From

- Communication Skills For Product Managers: The Communication Skills That Product Managers Need To Know How To Use In Order To Have A Successful Product

- How To Have A Successful Product Manager Career: The Things That You Need To Be Doing TODAY In Order To Have A Successful Product Manager Career

- Product Manager Product Success: How to keep your product on track and make it become a success

## Public Speaking

- Delivering Excellence: How To Give Presentations That Make A Difference: Presentation techniques that will transform a speech into a memorable event

- Tools Speakers Need In Order To Give The Perfect Speech: What tools to use to create your next speech so that your message will be remembered forever!

- How To Create A Speech That Will Be Remembered

- Secrets To Organizing A Speech For Maximum Impact: How to put together a speech that will capture and hold your audience's attention

- How To Become A Better Speaker By Changing How You Speak: Change techniques that will transform a speech into a memorable event

- How To Give A Great Presentation: Presentation techniques that will transform a speech into a memorable event

- How To Rehearse In Order To Give The Perfect Speech: How to effectively rehearse your next speech to that your message be remembered forever!

- Secrets To Creating The Perfect Speech: How to create a speech that will make your message be remembered forever!

- Secrets To Organizing The Perfect Speech: How to organize the best speech of your life!

- Secrets To Planning The Perfect Speech: How to plan to give the best speech of your life

- How To Show What You Mean During A Presentation: How to use visual techniques to transform a speech into a memorable event

## CIO Skills

- What CIOs Need To Know In Order To Successfully Manage An IT Department: Decision Making Skills That Every CIO Needs To Have In Order To Be Able To Make The Right Choices

- Becoming A Powerful And Effective Leader: Tips And Techniques That IT Managers Can Use In Order To Develop Leadership Skills

- CIO Secrets For Growing Innovation: Tips And Techniques For CIOs To Use In Order To Make Innovation Happen In Their IT Department

- Your Success As A CIO Depends On How Well You Communicate: Tips And Techniques For CIOs To Use In Order To Become Better Communicators

- What CIOs Need To Know About Working With Partners: Techniques For CIOs To Use In Order To Be Able To Successfully Work With Partners

- Critical CIO Management Skills: Decision Making Skills That Every CIO Needs To Have In Order To Be Able To Make The Right Choices

- How CIOs Can Make Innovation Happen: Tips And Techniques For CIOs To Use In Order To Make Innovation Happen In Their IT Department

- CIO Communication Skills Secrets: Tips And Techniques For CIOs To Use In Order To Become Better Communicators

- Managing Your CIO Career: Steps That CIOs Have To Take In Order To Have A Long And Successful Career

- CIO Business Skills: How CIOs can work effectively with the rest of the company!

## IT Manager Skills

- Save Yourself, Save Your Job – How To Manage Your IT Career: Secrets That IT Managers Can Use In Order To Have A Successful Career

- Growing Your CIO Career: How CIOs Can Work With The Entire Company In Order To Be Successful

- How IT Managers Can Make Innovation Happen: Tips And Techniques For IT Managers To Use In Order To Make Innovation Happen In Their Teams

- Staffing Skills IT Managers Must Have: Tips And Techniques That IT Managers Can Use In Order To Correctly Staff Their Teams

- Secrets Of Effective Leadership For IT Managers: Tips And Techniques That IT Managers Can Use In Order To Develop Leadership Skills

- IT Manager Career Secrets: Tips And Techniques That IT Managers Can Use In Order To Have A Successful Career

- IT Manager Budgeting Skills: How IT Managers Can Request, Manage, Use, And Track Their Funding

- Secrets Of Managing Budgets: What IT Managers Need To Know In Order To Understand How Their Company Uses Money

## Negotiating

- Learn How To Signal In Your Next Negotiation: How To Develop The Skill Of Effective Signaling In A Negotiation In Order To Get The Best Possible Outcome

- Learn The Skill Of Exploring In A Negotiation: How To Develop The Skill Of Exploring What Is Possible In A Negotiation In Order To Reach The Best Possible Deal

- Learn How To Argue In Your Next Negotiation: How To Develop The Skill Of Effective Arguing In A Negotiation In Order To Get The Best Possible Outcome|

- How To Open Your Next Negotiation: How To Start A Negotiation In Order To Get The Best Possible Outcome

- Preparing For Your Next Negotiation: What You Need To Do BEFORE A Negotiation Starts In Order To Get The Best Possible Deal

- Learn How To Package Trades In Your Next Negotiation

- All Good Things Come To An End: How To Close A Negotiation - How To Develop The Skill Of Closing

In Order To Get The Best Possible Outcome From A Negotiation

- Take No Prisoners In Your Next Negotiation: How To Start A Negotiation In Order To Get The Best Possible Outcome

## Miscellaneous

- How To Heal A Broken Leg – Fast!: Understanding how to deal with a broken leg in order to start walking again quickly

- How Software Defined Networking (SDN) Is Going To Change Your World Forever: The Revolution In Network Design  And How It Affects You

- The Power Of Virtualization: How It Affects Memory, Servers, and Storage: The Revolution In Creating Virtual Devices And How It Affects You

- The Internet-Enabled Successful School District Superintendent: How To Use The Internet To Boost Parental Involvement In Your Schools

- Power Distribution Unit (PDU) Secrets: What Everyone Who Works In A Data Center Needs To Know!

- Making The Jump: How To Land Your Dream Job When You Get Out Of College!

- How To Use The Internet To Create Successful Students And Involved Parents

*How To Develop The Skill Of Effective Arguing In A Negotiation In Order To Get The Best Possible Outcome*

This book has been written with one goal in mind – to show you how to successfully argue in your next negotiation. It's not easy being a negotiator and so we're going to show you how to successfully argue with the other side in order to get the deal that you want!

**Let's Make Your Negotiation A Success!**

**What You'll Find Inside:**

- **6 THINGS A SALES NEGOTIATOR NEEDS TO KNOW ABOUT USING THREATS DURING A NEGOTIATION**

- **GET WHAT YOU WANT BY BRINGING A PURPLE MONKEY TO YOUR NEXT NEGOTIATION**

- **LEGAL INTIMIDATION: 5 WAYS TO DEFEND AGAINST IT**

- **NEGOTIATORS NEED TO LEARN HOW TO DEAL WITH EXPERTS**

Dr. Jim Anderson brings his 25 years of real-world experience to this book. He's been a negotiator at some of the world's largest firms. He's going to show you what you need to do (and not do!) in order to get the best deal out of your next negotiation!

www.ingramcontent.com/pod-product-compliance
Lightning Source LLC
Chambersburg PA
CBHW061202180526
45170CB00002B/926